27.07   32

★ IT'S MY STATE! ★
Maine

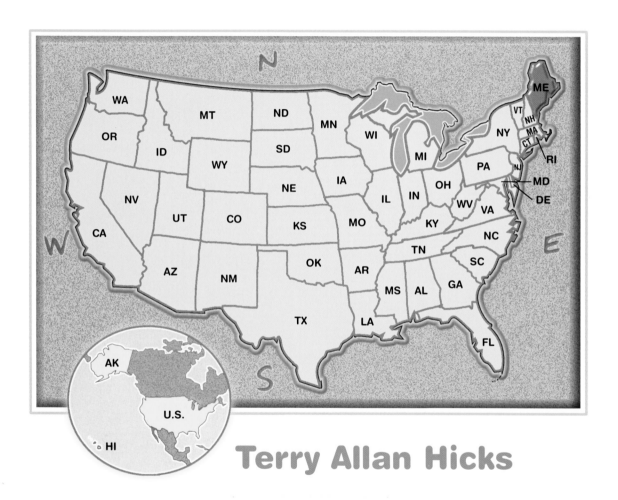

Terry Allan Hicks

 **Marshall Cavendish**
Benchmark
New York

3 9082 10365 9705

Marshall Cavendish Benchmark
99 White Plains Road
Tarrytown, New York 10591-9001
www.marshallcavendish.us

Maps, text, and illustrations copyright © 2006 by Marshall Cavendish Corporation
Illustrations and map on page 6 by Christopher Santoro
Map on page 75 by Ian Worpole

Library of Congress Cataloging-in-Publication Data

Hicks, Terry Allan.
Maine / by Terry Allan Hicks.
p. cm. -- (It's my state!)
Summary: "Surveys the history, geography, economy, and people of
Maine"--Provided by publisher.
Includes index.
ISBN 0-7614-1910-1
1. Maine--Juvenile literature. I. Title. II. Series.

F19.3.H53 2006
974.1--dc22
2005018058

Photo research by Candlepants Incorporated

Cover photograph: Comstock Images / PictureQuest

Back cover illustration: The license plate shows Maine's postal abbreviation followed by its year of statehood.

The photographs in this book are used by permission and through the courtesy of: Corbis: 22, 25, 35, 36, 52 (middle); Bettmann, 39, 40, 43 (top), 43 (bottom), 47, 53 (top); DK Limited, 5 (top); Joel W. Rogers, 15; Kevin Fleming, 17, 66; Richard Hamilton Smith, 19; Bob Krist, 44; W. Cody, 49; Neil Rabinowitz, 50, 64; Sygma, 52 (top); Oscar White 52 (bottom); Medford Historical Society, 53 (middle); Judy Griesedieck, 54, 55, 57, 69; Joseph Sohm / ChromoSohm Inc., 73 (middle). Northwind Picture Archives: 26, 28, 29, 30, 56. Envision: Mark Ferri, 68; Peter Johansky, 72 (middle); Andre Baranowski, 72 (bottom); Michael Kingsford, 73 (top); Deborah Burke, 73 (bottom). Minden Pictures: Tom Vezo, 4 (middle); Konrad Wothe, 5 (bottom); Tim Fitzharris, 10; Fred Bavendam, 18; YVA Momatiuk / John Eastcott, 20 (top); Mark Raycroft, 20 (middle); Frans Lanting, 21 (top); Eddy Marissen / Foto Natura, 21 (bottom). Animals Animals / Earth Scenes: John Lemker, 4 (top); Ted Levin, 4 (bottom), 20 (bottom); Bill Silliker, Jr., 5 (middle); EASTCOTT/MOMATIUK, 13; Michael Gadomski, 14; Cathy and Gordon Illg, 21 (middle); Jerry and Marcy Monkman, 42. SuperStock: Michael P. Gadomski, 8; Ron Dahlquist, 11; age footstock, 72 (top). AFP / Getty: 53 (bottom). The Image Works: Andre Jenny, 58. Maine State Museum, Augusta, Maine: 24.

Book design by Anahid Hamparian

Printed in Malaysia

1 3 5 6 4 2

Contents

A Quick Look at Maine

Nickname: The Pine Tree State
Population: 1,317,253 (2004 estimate)
Statehood: March 15, 1820

Tree: Eastern White Pine

This tough evergreen tree—also known as the northern white pine—has been the backbone of the Maine economy for hundreds of years. The tallest, straightest white pines in the Maine woods were once called "mast pines," because they were perfect for carrying ships' sails. The white pine was made the official state tree in 1945.

Bird: Black-Capped Chickadee

In 1927, Maine named the black-capped chickadee as the state bird. This small bird gets its name from its "chick-a-dee-dee" call. The black-capped chickadee is about 5 inches long and can be seen in the wooded areas and backyards of most Maine homes.

Fish: Landlocked Salmon

The landlocked salmon is a freshwater fish that can grow to weigh as much as 35 pounds. Maine named this salmon as its official fish in 1969. It is a natural resident of many of Maine's rivers, streams, and lakes. Fishermen across the state enjoy angling for the landlocked salmon.

Cat: Maine Coon Cat

This big cat originated in Maine, probably from different breeds of cat brought over by European settlers. Many Maine Coon cats have markings that make them look a little like raccoons, which is how they got their name. With their heavy fur, these cats are perfectly suited to cold Maine winters. A Maine Coon cat also has a bushy tail that it can wrap around itself to keep warm, and big round paws that work just like snowshoes. Maine Coon cats are larger and heavier than most other pet cats, but this breed is still very popular.

Animal: Moose

This large brown mammal is the largest member of the deer family found anywhere in the world. A male moose may be as tall as 6 feet at the shoulders and weigh 1,400 pounds. Male moose have antlers that can spread 5 feet across. Moose live around Maine's forests and fields and are often seen in backyards and on local roads. Maine made the moose its official state animal in 1979.

Insect: Honeybee

Maine's official state insect is the honeybee. Because the bees pollinate the flowers on plants and trees, the insects are important to orchards, farms, and gardens around the state. Honeybees also make sweet honey used and sold throughout Maine. The honeybee was named the official insect in 1975.

1 The Pine Tree State

New England is made up of six different states—Connecticut, Maine, Massachusetts, New Hampshire, Rhode Island, and Vermont. Maine is the largest of the New England states, and its total land area is almost as big as all of the other five states put together. But this 33,215-square-mile state is home to a surprisingly small number of people. The state population is around 1,300,000, which is smaller than the population of many of America's big cities. Some large parts of the state have almost no human residents.

The state's landscape and climate can make it a tough place to live. The coastline is rocky and jagged. The farmland in much of Maine is poor, and the growing season is short. Thick forests cover almost 90 percent of the Pine Tree State. The winters are long and cold. But these harsh conditions have made Maine residents—Mainers, as they are often called—a very special kind of people: tough, independent, and used to taking care of themselves. Most of the

Maine's Borders

North: Canada
South: Atlantic Ocean
East: Canada
West: New Hampshire and Canada

people who live in the state could not imagine living anywhere else. And a lot of "flatlanders"—people from outside the state—love Maine, too. Millions of visitors come to the state every year, making Maine one of the country's most popular tourist destinations.

The Coastal Lowlands

Maine can be divided into three main regions: the Coastal Lowlands, the New England Uplands, and the Great North Woods. The Coastal Lowlands is the land region covering the land that includes Maine's Atlantic coast. If you follow every twist and turn of the Maine coast, it is an amazing 3,478 miles, which is

West Penobscot Bay in Camden is a popular spot for sailing. Maine's numerous bodies of water are ideal for residents and visitors alike.

about as long as the California coast. This is "America's Playground," the Maine that many tourists know and love. Summer homes line the coast, from the Piscataqua River in the south to the Canadian

> More than sixty lighthouses are scattered along Maine's coastline. The oldest, Portland Head Light, was commissioned, or ordered built, by President George Washington in 1787. The lighthouse still shines brightly today.

border in the north. Visitors come here to the sun and sand at Old Orchard Beach and Ogunquit, eat lobster rolls and fried clams in little seaside restaurants, shop in the discount stores of Freeport, and photograph fishing villages and lighthouses that are many centuries old.

But the coastal lowlands are not just a playground. The sleek pleasure boats that glide through the water here pass working fishing boats. Every day of the year, in good weather and bad, Maine's fishermen are hard at work, hauling in lobsters from the offshore waters. They also net fish such as cod and haddock from farther out in the Gulf of Maine.

When the Ice Age ended about ten thousand years ago, the retreating glaciers left behind thousands of jagged inlets in the shoreline. The glaciers also created more than 2,000 islands, strung out like a jeweled necklace in the waters along the Maine coast. Only a few of these islands—like North Haven, in Penobscot Bay—are still home to year-round communities.

More than three thousand "summer people" spend part of the year on North Haven. But when the cold weather comes, the island's population drops to just three hundred. Holly Blake is one of the year-rounders. She teaches at the North Haven Community

School, one of only three island schools in Maine that still have classes from kindergarten to the twelfth grade under one roof. Ms. Blake says, "Island living takes a special kind of person. It's an hour's ride on the ferry just to get to the mainland, so you have to be able to take care of yourself. You also have to know how to get along with people, because this is such a close-knit community. After twelve years here, I really can't imagine a better place to live."

The most famous island in Maine is Mount Desert, home to Acadia National Park. The 100-square-mile Mount Desert is

The Atlantic coast can be seen from this part of Cadillac Mountain in Acadia National Park.

covered with tall peaks, including Cadillac Mountain. At 1,532 feet, this mountain is the highest point on the North Atlantic of the United States. It is said that if you stand at the top of Cadillac Mountain at daybreak, you will be the first person in the United States to see the sun rise. The town of Bar Harbor is also located on Mount Desert. This town is a popular tourist destination, but it is also a thriving seashore community.

Almost half of Maine's population lives within about 20 miles of the Atlantic Ocean. Portland, the state's largest city with more than 64,000 people, is found on the Atlantic coast, on beautiful, sweeping Casco Bay. Portland has been an important seaport

Waves crash against the coast beneath the historic Portland Head Light.

and shipbuilding center for centuries. Today, it also has high-tech industries and an international airport, as well. The greater Portland area, which includes the surrounding towns and cities, has a population of more than 240,000.

The New England Uplands

Just a few miles inland from the coast is the beginning of Maine's largest region, the New England Uplands. Here, the retreating glaciers left behind gently rolling hills, hundreds of rivers and thousands of lakes, and the best farmland in the state.

The Uplands are home to most of Maine's agriculture. The area around Augusta, the state capital, is dotted with apple orchards. In a good year, Maine produces more than 1.5 million bushels of apples. Many dairy farms also dot the Uplands. In the blueberry barrens in the northeastern corner of the state, Mainers harvest bushel after bushel of tiny, delicious wild blueberries.

Maine's most important agricultural area is Aroostook County, which Mainers call "The County," along the Canadian border. The County takes up 6,829 square miles, nearly a third of Maine's total area. Aroostook County is actually bigger than the states of Connecticut and Rhode Island put together.

The Uplands also have many industrial centers, such as the twin cities of Lewiston and Auburn. These cities face each other from opposite banks of the Androscoggin River. Together, they make up the state's second-largest city. Another important Upland town is Bangor, on the Penobscot River. Bangor is the heart of Maine's

The fruits that grow in Maine's wild blueberry fields are usually harvested in the fall by large machines.

all-important lumber industry. For many years, loggers floated fallen trees downriver to Bangor, where they were cut into boards for construction or mashed into pulp and paper.

Tourists come to the Uplands, too, to stay in little cabins—called "camps"—and enjoy fishing, hunting, canoeing, and hiking. Most of Maine's more than two thousand lakes and ponds are found here in the Uplands. This includes the biggest of them all, the 120-square-mile Moosehead Lake.

The Great North Woods

To the north and west of the Uplands is the region that shows most clearly why Maine is called the Pine Tree State. This area, the Great North Woods, is mostly untouched by human beings. It has been said that in the North Woods, a tree can grow, live, and die without ever being seen by a human being. The trees grow so thick and close here that, in many places, walking is nearly impossible.

The Longfellow Mountains run down through the heart of this region. These mountains are part of the much larger Appalachian Range. The highest of the Longfellows is Mount Katahdin. Katahdin is Maine's highest point and rises 5,268 feet—almost a mile—from a point close to sea level. Mount Katahdin is surrounded by Baxter State Park, a favorite spot for campers and hikers, and especially for people hiking on the Appalachian Trail. This is a

In 1936, a man named Myron Avery became the first person to walk the entire length of the Appalachian Trail. Since then, 7,736 "two-thousand-milers" have completed this grueling journey—including one man who did it at the age of seventy-nine!

long trail that runs for 2,174 miles, down through fourteen states. The trail ends at Springer Mountain in Georgia. An estimated three to four million people every year hike along different parts of the trail.

Mount Katahdin rises above Daicey Pond in Maine's Baxter State Park.

Many campers and kayakers enjoy the Great North Woods' natural beauty.

The Longfellow Mountains are great for winter sports, such as skiing on Sugarloaf Mountain, Maine's second-highest peak. High up in the Great North Woods, beyond the mountains, is another of Maine's hidden treasures: the Allagash Wilderness Waterway. The Allagash is a 92-mile chain of rivers and lakes that canoeists and whitewater kayakers love. It is also home to Maine's wildest wildlife. Evan Atkins, a visitor from Connecticut, learned that the hard way, while canoeing on the Allagash with a friend. "We saw a huge rock in the river ahead of us," he remembers. "We were paddling like crazy to keep from hitting it when the 'rock' raised its head and we realized it was a moose. I don't know who was more surprised—us or him!"

Climate

Six to eight months of the year, Maine's climate is mostly quite pleasant. Spring in Maine can be a delight. The summers are usually comfortable, too, with an average temperature throughout the state of 62 degrees Fahrenheit. But the temperature can drop suddenly, especially along the coast.

Many people believe autumn is the best time to be in Maine. When the temperature begins to fall, the leaves of this heavily wooded state turn to glorious reds, oranges, and yellows. But a Maine autumn can also have some dangers. Nor'easters are huge, violent storms that blow in from the Atlantic Ocean. These storms sometimes bring hurricane-force winds. When that happens, Mainers know the time has come to tie down their boats, board up the windows of their houses, and wait for the "blow" to end.

The great nor'easter of March 1993 was so powerful that it is known as the "storm of the century." More than two hundred people died in the storm, which struck the entire East Coast, from Maine all the way down to Florida.

There is no doubt about it, you have to be tough to make it through a Maine winter. The winters here can sometimes seem to last forever. In fact, winter weather conditions can last almost six months, from late November to early May. The Maine coast receives about 70 inches of snow during an average winter. Deep in the interior parts of the state, the snowfall is even heavier—about 100 inches.

The winters are cold, too. The average temperature along the coast in January is 20 degrees Fahrenheit. Inland, it is much, much colder, sometimes dropping to a

Maine winters are perfect for snowboarders and skiiers.

bone-chilling 8 degrees Fahrenheit. Maine's rivers and lakes, and even the harbors along the coast ice over, and it sometimes seems as if the state is coming to a standstill, just waiting for spring.

Life in the Wild

About half of Maine is completely uninhabited, and that makes it wonderful for wildlife. The skies above the coast are filled with hundreds of different species of birds, from bald eagles and ospreys to cormorants and puffins. The waters along the coast and around the offshore islands are home to five different kinds of seals. And below the surface of the water are lobsters, crabs, clams, mussels, scallops, shrimp, and sea urchins. The many species of fish include cod, flounder, and mackerel. A little farther out to the ocean, it is not unusual to see porpoises and whales breaking the surface.

The wolffish inhabits the ocean floor of Maine's Atlantic coast.

The mainland is home to a wonderful variety of wildlife—especially in the North Woods, far from civilization. Here, in the thick evergreen forests, black bears search for mountain cranberries, while moose nibble on water plants, and white-tailed deer shelter their young. The few people who travel through the woods may also see beavers, porcupines, snowshoe hares, and predators such as the Northern lynx.

This heavily forested state is covered with balsam, beech, birch, maple, oak, and, of course, pine trees. In the spring and summer, many parts of Maine are carpeted with wildflowers, including the black-eyed Susan, the lady's slipper, and a favorite of Mainers, the tall blue lupine. For those who know how to properly identify edible wild plants, some of Maine's plant life—including blueberries, cranberries, and fiddlehead ferns—can be very tasty.

The people of Maine live very close to nature, so they care deeply about preserving their natural environment. Mainers have created many laws and regulations to protect the land and wildlife of their state. Despite their efforts, however, many of Maine's species—from the golden eagle to the Katahdin Arctic butterfly—are still on the endangered species list. But with continuing efforts to protect the environment and Maine wildlife, Mainers hope that some of their state's endangered species can be brought back from the brink of extinction.

Mainers of all ages appreciate their state's natural beauty.

Plants & Animals

Atlantic Puffin

These odd-looking sea birds, with their big blue, red, and yellow beaks, almost disappeared from Maine in the 1800s. They were hunted for their feathers, which were used in ladies' hats. But beginning in 1973, a plan called Project Puffin helped them make a comeback, bringing baby puffins to live on some of Maine's offshore islands.

Black Bear

Black bears may weigh 600 pounds and measure 6 feet in length. But they can run surprisingly fast—up to 25 miles per hour. Black bears are very good tree-climbers. As many as 25,000 black bears roam the Maine woods, feeding on fish, nesting birds, blueberries, and wild honey.

Showy Lady's Slipper

These flowers can be found throughout the forests and fields of the Pine Tree State. A member of the orchid family, the showy lady's slipper was named for its distinctive shape—the flower resembles a lady's shoe. These blooms can come in a variety of colors, including yellow, pink, red, or purple.

Harbor Seal

Maine's fishermen used to shoot harbor seals, because they believed the seals stole the bait from their lobster traps. But environmental laws have helped to protect these migratory mammals, and more than 30,000 of them now make their home in Maine's waters.

Northern Lynx

This shy but fierce predator is one of the rarest sights in the Maine woods. But even though the lynx is considered a threatened species, some experts think there may be as many as 500 of them in the state. These tan, gray, and white cats feed on small mammals, birds, insects, and sometimes plants.

Lichen

Lichen—which is actually made up of two types of organisms, a fungus and algae—covers trees, rocks, and fence posts throughout the Maine woods. Lichens do not need any kind of food, only light, air, and rain, so they can often survive where almost no other life forms can. Many of Maine's wild animals, such as moose, birds, and deer, feed on lichen.

2 From the Beginning

People have lived in the land we now know as Maine for more than 10,000 years. Very little is known about the first of these early Native Americans, who are called Paleo-Indians. But they probably hunted caribou and other large animals by using stone weapons.

A new group of Native Americans appeared about 2500 BCE. They are known as the Red Paint People because they buried their dead in graves lined with stones colored with red clay. They seem to have disappeared by about 1800 BCE. Centuries later, probably between 500 CE and 1000 CE, another group of Native Americans were living along the coast. These people are thought to have been fishermen, because they left behind huge mounds of oyster shells.

The People of the Dawn

By the fourteenth century—and perhaps much earlier—Maine was home to a new group of Native Americans, the Abenaki. The

Children with American flags participate in a Memorial Day parade in Ashland around 1943.

name Abenaki means "people of the dawn." The Abenaki are part of the much larger Algonquian group, which includes peoples who lived as far apart as Nova Scotia and California.

More than twenty different Abenaki groups lived in Maine, including the Penobscot, the Passamaquoddy, and the Micmac. There were many differences among these groups. The Passamaquoddy, who lived in northeastern Maine, were mostly hunters. The Penobscot were farmers, growing corn and beans on the fertile farmland of the central coast.

For centuries, the Abenaki fought their traditional enemies, the Iroquois, who lived to the north and the west of them. By the 1600s, war had weakened the Abenaki, making it difficult for them to face a new threat—the arrival of Europeans.

The Abenaki were some of the firs Native Americans to live in the region that includes present-day Maine.

Explorers and Settlers

The first white people who visited Maine were probably Vikings. The Vikings were warriors from Norway and Denmark. They sailed their longships down the coast of North America from Greenland to the area that is now the Carolinas, perhaps as early as 700 CE.

Beginning in the 1500s, other European explorers began visiting Maine. Giovanni Caboto, an Italian sea captain who worked for the English may have sailed along the coast in 1497. He is also known by his English name, John Cabot. In 1524, another Italian explorer, Giovanni da Verrazano, landed at Casco Bay, near present-day Portland. He claimed the land for the

This painting is an artist's impression of John Cabot landing in the region.

European explorers paddled through the region's rivers, lakes, and bays, as they charted the land for France and England.

French. The first European visitors described Maine as beautiful but dangerous. Verrazano and the Abenaki did not get along, and he called the region "the Land of the Bad People."

The first European attempt to settle in Maine ended in disaster. In 1604, Pierre du Gua—part of a French expedition led by the explorer Samuel de Champlain—built a small outpost at the mouth of the Saint Croix River. The place was called Île des Monts Déserts. We know it today as Mount Desert Island. Champlain kept going, up the Penobscot River as far as where Bangor is today. When he returned the following spring, he found more than half of Gua's men dead or dying, most from a disease called

Nobody knows for certain where the name "Maine" comes from. Some people think the early explorers named it for the French "Province of Maine." But it may just mean "the mainland."

scurvy, which is caused by a poor diet.

The French never again tried to settle in Maine, but they did not really leave, either. They worked closely with the Abenaki in the fur trade, becoming their closest allies. This would later cause great problems for the next group to settle in Maine: the English.

A Century of War

The English were living in Maine as early as 1607. Their settlements included York—the first legally chartered town in what was to become the United States—Biddeford, Saco, and Falmouth. These were mostly trading posts, where the English bought fish, wood, and furs from the Native Americans.

In 1622, the British king granted a huge piece of land in New England to two English noblemen, Sir Ferdinando Gorges and John Mason. Seven years later, the two men split up the land, with Gorges taking the northern section, which was the part that became Maine. (Mason's share is now the state of New Hampshire.) In 1652, the small, scattered settlements of Maine came under the control of the older, more established Massachusetts Bay Colony.

The English soon came into conflict with the French, who also wanted to control Maine and its rich resources. In 1689, the English settlers began fighting a long series of wars against the French and their Abenaki allies. These conflicts, known as the French and Indian Wars, lasted almost a century.

The capture of the great French fortress at Louisbourg, in present-day Nova Scotia, in 1745 was a turning point in the French and Indian Wars. The raiding party was led by a Mainer—William Pepperrell of Kittery.

European settlers found the region plentiful in lumber and seafood.

By this time, most of New England was peaceful and prosperous. But Maine was still the wild frontier, where farmhouses and villages were sometimes attacked and burned to the ground.

Life was hard for the settlers of early Maine—but it was far harder for the Native Americans. Many of them died from war and disease, and many others fled the fighting to live in the French-controlled areas in Canada. Things became especially bad for them after 1763, when the French signed a treaty that gave Britain control of most of their possessions in North America.

By the time the French and Indian Wars came to an end, about 24,000 people were living in Maine. Settlers were moving inland, clearing the forests to create farmland. This was a time of peace in Maine, but it did not last long.

Many people in the colonies hated British rule. The colonists had to pay high taxes, but felt they had no voice in their government. Opposition to British rule led to the

One British law that Mainers hated was the "ship's mast law." It said all white pines more than 24 inches across belonged to the king—to be used as masts for British navy ships.

Revolutionary War. Mainers played an important role before and during the war. They burned British tea shipments in York in 1774, in an incident known as the "York Tea Party." They also acted out against the British in Falmouth in 1775.

When the Revolutionary War started in 1775, the people of Maine fought hard on the side of independence. The first naval battle of the war was in 1775, near Machias, when Mainers seized a British ship called the *Margaretta*. The Mainers were good at using their knowledge of the land to their advantage. They

Ships burn in Falmouth. The Revolutionary War would soon affect all of the colonies.

sometimes extinguished the signals in the lighthouses along the coast, which made the British ships run onto the rocks.

Maine paid a high price for rebelling against the British. In 1775, Falmouth was attacked with cannon fire. Hundreds of buildings were burned to the ground, and most of the ships in the harbor were sunk. When the war ended in 1783, Maine worked hard to recover. Falmouth was one of the rebuilt cities. Part of it later became Portland. Maine's shipyards hummed with activity, as timber from the state's pine forests was sawed and hammered to make wooden sailing ships.

As Europeans took control of more land, they started cutting down the regions forests. The lumber from the plentiful forests helped to make the region's logging industry very profitable.

Many new settlers arrived in Maine, as huge pieces of land—totaling about 12.5 million acres—were taken from the Passamaquoddy and Penobscot and given to veterans of the Revolutionary War. For a time, the Pine Tree State was prosperous and peaceful. But once again, Maine's good times were shattered by war. Mainers were almost as unhappy with the state government in Massachusetts as they had been with their British rulers. This turned into great bitterness during the War of 1812, a conflict between Britain and the new United States.

The British took control of a long stretch of the northern Maine coast, from Belfast to Eastport, close to the Canadian border. They cut off all contact with the outside world, and the Maine economy suffered terribly. Maine asked Massachusetts for help—but no help came. When the War of 1812 ended, the people of Maine demanded statehood. On March 15, 1820, they got their wish. Maine became the twenty-third state in the Union, and Portland was named its capital. The capital was moved inland, to Augusta, in 1832, so that people from the northern parts of the state could visit their lawmakers more easily.

The newly independent state was bustling with life. Ships from all over the world filled Maine's harbors, their cargo holds waiting to carry away the state's products: fish, timber, and stone. They even carried blocks of ice—cut from frozen rivers and packed in sawdust to keep from melting—to chill food in those days before refrigerators.

In 1839, the United States and Britain almost went to war yet again, over the rich timberlands of northern Maine. A treaty ended the so-called "Aroostook War" in 1842.

Making a Punched Picture

Many colonists decorated their homes with objects made out of punched tin. Sometimes they had punched-tin lanterns or candle holders. They also hung punched-tin pictures on their wall. Following these simple instructions, you can make your own punched-tin picture.

Materials You Will Need

1 aluminum pie plate
1 nail
A hammer
Piece of plain paper
Pen
Scotch tape or masking tape

You will need an adult to help you use the hammer and nail for this project.

Draw a simple design or picture on the paper. Make sure your design will fit within the borders of the bottom of the pie plate.

Tape the paper to the pie plate, making sure your design is centered.

Put the pie plate on a work surface, such as a large scrap of wood or very thick cardboard. (You should ask an adult where you can put the pie plate because you do not want to damage the floor, a table, or a countertop.)

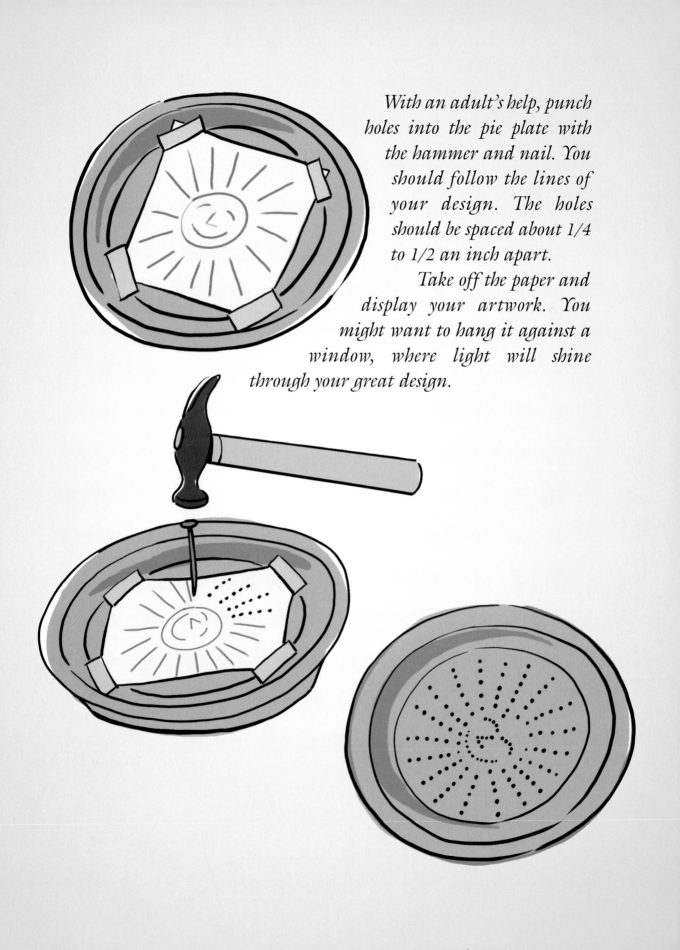

With an adult's help, punch holes into the pie plate with the hammer and nail. You should follow the lines of your design. The holes should be spaced about 1/4 to 1/2 an inch apart.

Take off the paper and display your artwork. You might want to hang it against a window, where light will shine through your great design.

By the mid-1800s, mill towns were springing up all over the Maine Uplands. The rushing waters of the Androscoggin and other rivers powered sawmills, textile mills, and shoe factories. And the mills gave work to immigrants, who were beginning to arrive in Maine in large numbers for the first time. Life was good for many Americans until the Civil War began.

The Civil War and Beyond

By the 1850s, Americans were divided over the issue of slavery. Many states, especially in the South, allowed whites to own African Americans as slaves. But most New Englanders hated this practice. When Maine became a state, one of its first official acts was to outlaw slavery. The fight against slavery became a great cause for millions of Americans. Some people believe one of the turning points came when a preacher's wife in Brunswick, Maine, sat down to write a book. Her name was Harriet Beecher Stowe, and the book was *Uncle Tom's Cabin*. This novel described the mistreatment of southern plantation slaves, and their attempts to escape to the free states in the North. The book was a sensation, selling more than 300,000 copies in its first year. It helped to open the world's eyes to the evils of slavery.

In 1861, when the North and South could not resolve their differences, they finally went to war. The Civil War lasted four long years, and cost nearly 400,000 Americans their lives. An estimated 70,000 Mainers fought on the Northern, or Union, side. At the Battle of

In 1862, at the height of the Civil War, Harriet Beecher Stowe visited President Abraham Lincoln at the White House. When he met her, the president said, "So you're the little woman who wrote the book that started this great war."

Though no Civil War battles were fought in Maine, many residents volunteered to fight for the Uuion.

Gettysburg, the Twentieth Maine Regiment, outnumbered two to one by the Southern forces, fought until they ran out of ammunition. Then they charged with bayonets, forcing the Southerners to retreat. This turned the tide in one of the greatest battles of the Civil War. Though none of its battles were fought in Maine, the Civil War took a terrible toll on the state. More than 7,000 of Maine's young men died serving their country.

In the late 1800s through the early 1900s, even very young children were expected to work. Unfortunately, many of these jobs had very dangerous working conditions.

Maine

The years after the war brought great changes to Maine. The age of the wooden ship was coming to an end, as sailing ships were replaced by metal ships powered by steam. The demand for Maine timber decreased. But Mainers adapted. The state's shipyards, especially in Bath, near the mouth of the Kennebec River, began building metal ships—a practice that is still continues today.

Maine found new uses for its trees, too. Books and newspapers were becoming more common—because more people knew how to read—and their publishers needed a steady supply of paper. Pulp and paper mills were built all across northern Maine, to crush wood into pulp and then turn it into paper.

These growing industries needed more and more workers, and most of them came from other countries. Many of these immigrants came from Ireland, and they gave many parts of Maine Irish place names, such as Belfast. Others came from Sweden to clear farmland in Aroostook Country, and from Finland to work in the stone quarries along the coast. In 1870, fifty-one Swedish immigrants built a town in Aroostook Country. Just ten years later, almost 800 people lived in the so-called "colony" of New Sweden.

The largest group of new arrivals came from land much closer to Maine—the nearby Canadian provinces of New Brunswick and Quebec. These French-speaking immigrants mostly came to work in mills and factories. They were promised that they could keep their language, their culture, and their religion. For many years, the French-Canadians of Maine kept themselves somewhat separate from other Mainers, living and working in "petits Canadas" ("little Canadas"), with their own schools, churches, and businesses.

During this time, Maine's tourist industry was beginning to

grow. The town of Bar Harbor, on Mount Desert Island, became a fashionable summer resort for the wealthy, who built huge seaside mansions for themselves and their summer guests. By the 1880s, there were at least thirty hotels in Bar Harbor.

Soon, steamships and railways were bringing in less wealthy visitors. They first came to spend summers on the coast, in places such as Kennebunk and Camden. Then resorts began to open on Moosehead and other lakes in the interior. Maine's resorts began to be important source of jobs for Mainers.

The Bath Iron Works launched its first ship in 1890. Since then, more than 400 new vessels have been built at the shipyard, including 245 U.S. Navy ships.

Modern Maine

By the beginning of the twentieth century, Maine was a somewhat different place from what it had once been. The state's population had grown to about 700,000. As newcomers to the state—both immigrants and "summer people"—became more commonplace, Mainers worried about how to preserve the things that made their state special. This has been one of Maine's greatest concerns ever since.

The new century was not always easy for Maine. When the United States entered World War I, in 1917, Maine sent about 35,000 soldiers to fight on the battlefields of France. During the war, the state was able to earn some money providing supplies for the war effort. But after the war, the supplies were no longer needed, causing great hardship in the state.

It was during this period that the people of Maine first began taking steps to protect their natural environment. In

1919, the United States Congress created Acadia National Park—the first national park east of the Mississippi River. Beginning in 1931, Percival Baxter, an ex-governor, began donating thousands of acres of land around Mount Katahdin. This wilderness area became Baxter State Park.

But in the 1920s and 1930s, Mainers were mostly concerned with economic survival. Times were hard, and they got even worse during the Great Depression. This was a period of economic hardship, beginning in 1929, that created poverty and unemployment all over the country.

During the Depression, the federal government created a make-work project called the Civilian Conservation Corps

Stores and businesses across the nation closed down during the Great Depression. Many were left with no money, no homes, and no jobs.

To help with the war effort, many women worked in factories. These factories made supplies that were used by the soldiers fighting in World War II.

 Maine

(CCC). In Maine, the CCC gave about 20,000 people jobs building public works projects, such as hiking trails through the North Woods. CCC workers completed the Appalachian Trail in 1937.

It was only in the early 1940s—when the United States entered World War II—that Maine's economy began to improve. Demand for the state's natural resources and manufactured goods increased. Casco Bay was the headquarters for the U.S. Navy ships fighting German submarines in the North Atlantic. The shipyards of the coast were working day and night, as welders and mechanics built destroyers at the Bath Iron Works and submarines at the Portsmouth Naval Shipyard.

For several decades after the end of World War II, Maine's economy was strong, and the state's workers had little trouble finding jobs. But then, in the late 1970s, that began to change. The traditional Maine industries began to face growing competition from other parts of the country, and other parts of the world. And two important concerns of Mainers—making a living and protecting the environment—began to come into conflict.

Environmentalists had been asking for laws to protect Maine's land and wildlife for a long time. But many Mainers worried that these laws would cost jobs. In the 1970s, for example, clear-cutting, which is a logging method that cuts down all the trees in an area, was banned along Maine's rivers. It was thought to be harmful to the fish that live in the rivers, especially the landlocked salmon. But when environmentalists tried to stop clear-cutting everywhere in the state, the proposal was defeated. Many people were afraid it would hurt the lumber industry.

Even today the Maine economy faces some tough times. Different industries from agriculture to manufacturing are having problems remaining successful. Many Mainers are worried about their jobs. Many are also worried about preserving the natural environment and the traditional Maine way of life because they fear that environmental laws could cost more jobs. These sometimes-conflicting concerns have been Mainers' greatest concerns for more than a century—and probably will be for a long time to come. But with time and effort, Mainers will find a way to endure and progress as they have for centuries.

For more than two centuries, the Portsmouth Naval Shipyard, at the mouth of the Piscataqua River, was part of New Hampshire. But in 2001, the Supreme Court ended a long "border dispute" between the two states by saying it belonged to Maine.

Fort Foster is a historic fort located on the Piscataqua River near Kittery. It is an example of how Mainers work hard to treasure and learn from their state's past.

Important Dates

2500 BCE-1500 CE Maine is inhabited by a series of Native American peoples—the Paleo-Indians, the Red Paint People, the "oyster mound people," and finally the Abenaki.

700 CE -1524 European navigators, including Vikings and the Italians Giovanni Caboto and Giovanni da Verrazano, sail along the Maine coast.

1604 The French build the first European settlement in Maine, but are forced to abandon it.

1622 The British king grants "the province of Maine" to Sir Ferdinando Gorges and John Mason, who in 1629 divide it into Maine and New Hampshire.

1689-1763 The English fight the French and their Native American allies in the French and Indian Wars.

Harriet Beecher Stowe

1774-1775 The American Revolution comes to Maine, with rioting in York and Falmouth, and naval engagements in Machias and Castine.

1820 Maine becomes the twenty-third state, with Portland as its capital.

1852 Harriet Beecher Stowe publishes *Uncle Tom's Cabin*, a novel that focuses the world's attention on the slavery issue.

1861-1865 Maine fights on the Northern side in the Civil War.

1880s Bar Harbor becomes a fashionable resort town, marking the beginning of Maine's tourist industry.

1928 Acadia National Park is created on Mount Desert Island.

1937 The Appalachian Trail is completed by federal government "make-work" crews.

1940 and 1948 Mainer Margaret Chase Smith is elected to the United States House of Representatives and later the Senate, becoming the first woman to be elected to both houses of Congress.

Margaret Chase Smith

1980 The federal courts award the Penobscot and Passamoquoddy tribes $81.5 million in compensation for the Maine land taken from them after the American Revolution.

2001 A Supreme Court decision returns the Portsmouth Naval Shipyards to Maine, ending a two-hundred-year dispute with New Hampshire.

3 The People

Maine's long history has made it a very distinctive place, with strong traditions and customs. And Mainers are very proud of the way of life in the Pine Tree State. The hardships of life in Maine have made many of the state's communities very close-knit. People there are ready to help when a neighbor has a problem. "Many winter nights I've come home from working the late shift to find somebody's plowed my driveway for me," says Leon Seamon, a retired pulp mill worker from Jay, near the state capital. "Never found out who's done it. It's just the way people are around here."

In some ways, Maine is less diverse than many other states. About 98 percent of Mainers are white. The largest single ethnic group in the state is people of British ancestry—just as it has been since the eighteenth century.

But this does not mean that everybody in the Pine Tree State is the same. One of the most important ethnic groups in the state is people of French-Canadian ancestry. They now

Maine's coasts have long attracted new residents.

represent about one-quarter of Maine's population. To this day, you will hear French spoken—with a strong Canadian accent—on the streets of Lewiston and Biddeford. Maine's French-Canadians worked hard to preserve their traditional language and culture, and their historical ties with Canada. Some of the highlights of a summer visit to Maine are festivals that celebrate the vibrant French-Canadian culture, with fiddle music, folk dancing, and food.

One ethnic group that has had a very difficult time in Maine is the Native Americans. Before Europeans came to the region, the

In 1755, French-Canadians began settling in Maine's St. John Valley, when the British forced them to leave their homes in New Brunswick and Nova Scotia, which they called Acadia. Many other Acadians went to Louisiana, where they became known as Cajuns—and they still speak French.

entire population was Native American. Now, Native Americans make up less than 1 percent of the Maine's population. Many of the Abenaki of Maine live on reservations with high unemployment and poor living conditions. But in recent years, they have worked hard to improve living conditions on their reservations, and to revive their language and their traditional crafts. Not all Natives living in Maine are on reservations. Many live in the state's towns and cities, working, going to school, and playing alongside Mainers of different ethnic backgrounds. Wherever they live, Maine's Native American populations continue to honor their heritage through traditional celebrations and festivals held throughout much of the state.

This Penoboscot family poses for a photograph in the early 1900s. Though they were the first residents to live in the region, they now represent a very small portion of the popultion.

In 1980, a federal court ruled that land belonging to Maine's Native Americans had been taken illegally in the eighteenth century. The Penobscot and Passamoquoddy tribes were awarded $81.5 million in payments for their land.

Despite the arrival of French-Canadians and others, Maine still has fewer immigrants than most states. By the beginning of the twenty-first century, only about 4 percent of the people living in Maine were born in other countries. That is a much smaller number than the national average. But that, like many things about Maine, is slowly changing.

In Portland, especially, new arrivals from other countries are beginning to transform the city's downtown area.

People from countries as far away as Yemen, Iran, and Vietnam are bringing their own cultures and traditions to the state. They open shops, restaurants, and other businesses. Changes are not just happening on the seacoast. Cities and towns inland also have some newcomers from other countries. But not all of these newcomers are from other countries. Through the years, many people from different states have made Maine their home.

> *We stand united as one in Maine when it comes to neighborliness, when it comes to tolerance, when it comes to opportunity."*
> —Governor John Baldacci of Maine, addressing a rally against racism in Lewiston

Changing Times

People sometimes say there are really "two Maines." What they mean is that the seacoast is, in some ways, very different from the interior. The most important difference is in economic opportunity—and especially jobs.

The seacoast has always been more prosperous than the inland areas of the state because it has more contact with the outside world. In recent years, the division between the two Maines has become even greater than in the past. Many wealthy people have moved to the seacoast bringing more money to the region, while the resource-based industries of the interior have

The small town of Camden is a mixture of modern buildings and historic architecture.

declined. The result is that the people who live on the seacoast have more jobs, and their jobs pay better.

This has caused a serious change in the state's population levels. Maine's overall population has increased steadily for hundreds of years. But in some parts of northern Maine, such as Aroostook and Androscoggin counties, the population is now declining. This is because young people often have to move elsewhere to find good jobs.

Even on the seacoast, the arrival of more people and the money they bring with them, is forcing Mainers to make difficult choices. A landowner may be tempted to sell property that has belonged to his family for generations, because the demand for land for houses is so great. The pressure is especially strong along the waterfront. A small home on waterfront property

Most of Maine's population is of European descent.

may sell for a million dollars or more, and a simple Maine house may be torn down to make way for a huge summer home.

Sally Merchant, whose family has lived in Maine since the 1700s, has watched the changes in the coast for many years. She and her husband run a landing for pleasure boaters and commercial fisherman at Spruce Head, on Penobscot Bay. "Waterfront property along here is being bought up at prices local people just can't afford to pay," she says. "All in all, that might be good for the local economy—but it sometimes means a fisherman doesn't have a place to dock his boat and sell his catch."

One of the most interesting government projects in recent years is an attempt to bring the "two Maines" together, using technology. Many people in Maine worry that their children are receiving an unequal education. The schools in the wealthier towns of the seacoast can afford many things—such as up-to-date computers—but areas with less money cannot.

In 2001, Maine's decided to undertake an ambitious project to bridge this "digital divide." This project, the Wired Maine initiative, promises to give every student in the state access to computers and the Internet. So far, almost $40 million has been spent, and every Maine seventh-grader has received a state-of-the-art "laptop" computer with wireless Internet access. This is probably the most money any state has ever spent to buy technology for its students.

It is too early to tell whether this project will result in Maine's students—especially in the less prosperous parts of the state—becoming more technologically advanced and better-educated. But Wired Maine does show that Mainers are always willing to try new ways to solve problems and make life in their state better.

The Arts in Maine

One group of people who have never been in short supply in Maine is artists. Writers, painters, and many other kinds of artists have always been drawn to the spectacular landscape and fascinating traditions of the Pine Tree State. Many came to Maine from elsewhere, but a large number were born in the state.

Famous Mainers

Stephen King: Writer

One of the most famous writers in the world, Stephen King was born in Portland and has lived almost his entire life in Maine. More than 300 million copies of his novels of horror and suspense have been published, and many have been made into popular movies. Some of his best-known books—including Carrie, Christine, and Cujo—are set in the little towns of Maine.

Dorothea Dix: Activist

Dorothea Dix was born in Hampden in 1802 and is famous for fighting for better care for the mentally ill. Dix traveled across the country and observed the terrible conditions in which these people lived. She helped to bring this issue to the public's attention and asked states to provide money to create better mental institutions. Dorothea Dix also supervised Union nurses during the Civil War.

Andrew Wyeth: Artist

Three generations of Wyeths have spent their lives painting in Maine. N. C. Wyeth, one of the greatest magazine illustrators of his day, moved to Port Clyde in 1910. His son Andrew is in his eighties, but is still painting the people and places around Cushing. And his son Jamie—who lives part of the year in a lighthouse on an island in Penobscot Bay—is following in the family tradition.

Henry Wadsworth Longfellow: Poet

Henry Wadsworth Longfellow is considered one of the greatest American poets. Longfellow was born in Portland in 1807 and grew up in Maine. He also attended Maine's well-respected Bowdoin College. Longfellow's works such as "The Song of Hiawatha" and "The Courtship of Miles Standish" are thought of as American masterpieces. In his work, Longfellow used themes that included the American landscape and Native American culture.

Hannibal Hamlin: Politician

Hannibal Hamlin was born in 1809 in Paris, Maine. Hamlin was the first Mainer to serve as vice president of the United States. In the 1840s he served in the United States House of Representatives and the Senate. Hamlin was opposed to slavery and was chosen to run alongside Abraham Lincoln in 1860 during the presidential election. Lincoln became president and Hamlin served as his vice president.

Joan Benoit Samuelson: Athlete

Samuelson is a famous athlete from Freeport. She won a gold medal at the 1984 Olympic Summer Games in the women's marathon event. This was the first time this event was held at the Olympics. Samuelson has also run in popular marathons in cities such as Boston and Chicago. While she was competing, she also had some of the fastest times in women's marathons. Today she works for many charitable causes and has coached other runners of all ages. Samuelson has also established a world-class road race in her home state, which benefits many of Maine's children's charities.

Henry Wadsworth Longfellow, born in Portland in 1807, is a famous American poet. His best-known poem, "Evangeline," tells the tragic story of the French-Canadians who were uprooted by the British and forced to move to America. Other great Maine poets were Edna St. Vincent Millay of Rockland, and Edward Arlington Robinson, who was born in Alna. The most popular Maine writer today is the horror novelist Stephen King. He was born in Portland, and he still spends much of the year in Bangor. Maine also gave Hollywood one of its greatest artists—the director John Ford. Even though he came from the seacoast town of Cape Elizabeth, Ford is best known for his classic Westerns, which often starred the famous actor John Wayne.

Painters, too, have always been drawn to Maine, and especially to the breathtaking scenery of the seacoast. Winslow

Maine's dramatic coastline and natural beauty have long been inspirations for writers, painters, and other artists.

Homer, one of the most famous artists of nineteenth-century America, spent many years depicting the seascapes. In the mid-twentieth century, Rockwell Kent became famous for his paintings of Monhegan Island, where he lived for many years. The Wyeth family—N.C., Andrew, and Jamie—have been painting in Maine for almost a hundred years.

No matter where they are from or what they do, Mainers are proud to call the state their home. Its beautiful land, bustling cities, good schools, charming towns, and good-hearted people all make the Pine Tree State a great place to live.

Mainers watch fireworks light the night sky during a festival honoring their state's culture and history.

Calendar of Events

National Toboggan Championships

During the first weekend in February, Camden plays host to hundreds of thrill-seeking tobogganers. The heart-stopping dash down the 400-foot toboggan "chute" takes about ten seconds and an awful lot of courage.

Maine Maple Sunday

On the fourth Sunday in March, sugar houses all over the state open their doors to visitors. You can watch 40 gallons of tree sap being turned into 1 gallon of maple syrup—and, of course, you can have a taste of this sweet treat.

Annual Windjammer Days

For one weekend in June, Boothbay Harbor is crowded with windjammers and other "tall ships," just like in the old days.

Acadian Festival

The largest cultural festival in Maine happens in late June, in Madawaska, high up on the Canadian border. Every year, the highlight of the festival is a huge reunion of one of Maine's pioneering Acadian families.

A parade

Indian Days

This celebration of Maine's Native American heritage is held in July on the Passamaquoddy reservation at Pleasant Point, near Eastport. The highlights include traditional crafts, drumming, and canoe races.

Maine Lobster Festival

Every August, some 80,000 lobster lovers descend on Rockland. They come to enjoy parades, music, and, of course, about 25,000 pounds' worth of lobsters.

Maine Wild Blueberry Festival

The sweetest place in all of Maine may just be the little town of Union. Union celebrates the August blueberry harvest with muffins, cakes, pastries, and nearly four thousand of the best pies you'll ever taste.

York Harvestfest

Autumn is wonderful time to visit the historic village of York, which celebrates the coming of autumn with traditional Maine handicrafts, wagon rides, and historical reenactments.

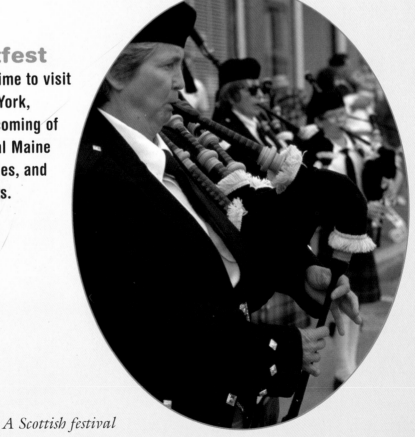

A Scottish festival

4 How It Works

The famous independent spirit of the Pine Tree State shows clearly in the way Mainers govern themselves. The people of Maine make up their own minds about the political issues of the day—and when they want something to happen, they often make it happen themselves.

Maine is represented in the federal government, in Washington, D.C., by two senators and two members of the House of Representatives. Maine's senators are elected to six-year terms by all the voters of the state, while members of the House of Representatives serve for two years at a time.

The Maine constitution, which was adopted in 1820, divides the state government into three separate but equal branches: executive, legislative, and judicial. This arrangement creates a balance of powers, so that one branch will not become stronger than the others.

The people elected to represent Maine are often every bit as independent as the people who sent them there. But it is at the local, or municipal, level that Maine's unique brand of self-

Maine's state legislature meets at the capitol in Augusta.

Branches of Government

Executive The executive branch—headed by the governor—makes certain that the state's laws are carried out properly, and handles the day-to-day running of the state government. The governor is elected by all the voters of the state, in elections held every four years, and can serve no more than two terms in a row.

Legislative The Maine legislature is divided into two houses: the senate and the house of representatives, which meet at the State House in Augusta. The 35 members of the Senate, and the 151 members of the House of Representatives, create new laws and change existing ones. They are elected by their local districts, and serve for two-year terms.

Judicial The judicial branch—the court system—settles legal disputes, punishes people who commit crimes, and decides whether Maine's laws violate the state constitution. The seven judges on the Supreme Judicial Court handle the most serious cases and constitutional issues. The superior court handles major criminal trials and lawsuits. Lower courts—including district, juvenile, and family courts—deal with other matters. All of Maine's judges are appointed by the state's governor, and serve terms of seven years.

government shows most clearly. Maine's has 16 counties, 22 cities, and 435 towns. Under a special form of government called home rule each local area has the right to choose its own form of local government.

Some of Maine's cities and town have an elected mayor and a city or town council. These officials make important decisions about the management of the area. But most of Maine's communities are run by representatives called selectmen (even though they can be either men or women). The selectmen handle the day-to-day running of the town. But the most important decisions are made at a town meeting.

An important and independent-minded Maine political figure is William Cohen, from Bangor. He was a congressman and senator, but also served as secretary of defense under President Bill Clinton. After retiring from politics, Cohen helped bring about a peaceful settlement to the long, bitter conflict between Catholics and Protestants in Northern Ireland.

The town meeting has been a New England tradition for hundreds of years. Once a year, all the residents of a town can come to the annual meeting, to discuss and vote on the most important local political issues. This is one of the oldest forms of direct democracy in the world, and it gives everyone in the town a voice in their government.

In the past, just about everybody came to the town meeting. Geoff Parker, a selectman in Rockport, says that has changed. "Sometimes no more than thirty or forty people come to the town meeting," he says. That might not seem like very many people, when you consider that Rockport has a population of over three thousand. But the town meetings are now shown live on television and, Geoff points out, "The next day, everybody in town seems to have watched it."

The Maine state elections of 1920 were the first elections in the United States in which women were allowed to vote.

How a New Law Is Created

The process of creating a new law is a slow, careful one. A new Maine law begins as an idea that is proposed by one of the members of either house of the state legislature. The member proposes the creation of a new law, and lawyers, researchers and other legislature staff help write a draft version of the proposed law. This draft is called a bill.

The bill is then sent to a committee made up of members of the house or senate. The committee recommends that the law be presented to the full house or sends it back for more consideration. Sometimes the house and senate disagree on what form a bill should take. If this happens, the bill is sent to another committee, which tries to work out a compromise version. Finally, the bill is sent to both houses for a vote. If it receives a majority of votes in both houses, it is referred to the governor to sign.

If the governor signs the bill, it becomes law. However, the governor may refuse to sign it. This is called a veto, and keeps the law from taking effect. The legislature can override this veto, with a two-thirds majority vote in both houses. If it does, the bill becomes a law even though the governor disagrees with it

How You Can Make a Difference

If there is a political issue that you care about, you really can make a difference. Many of Maine's laws were created because ordinary Mainers wanted them.

The first step is to make sure you are well-informed about all sides of the issues. You can do this by reading your local newspaper, following the news on television or radio, or visiting appropriate news sites on the Internet. Your school and local libraries also have many books and publications that can give you the information you need.

The next thing to do is to find out how to contact your elected representatives. You can probably find the leaders of your local government—the mayor, the city council members, or the selectmen—listed in the telephone book. If you have access to the Internet, finding your state representatives is easy. Most states have Web sites that give the names, addresses, telephone numbers and e-mail addresses of its members, and some even say how they have voted on many political issues. All you need to know to find your legislator is the name of the city, town, or county you live in.

Now that you know who your representatives are, it is time to make your voice heard. If you live in a town that holds an annual town meeting, you can attend it, even if you are not old enough to vote. It is always very interesting to hear your neighbors talk about the things that matter most to them. And it is especially interesting to realize how many of those things directly affect you.

To find contact information for Maine's state senators, visit this Web site:
http://janus.state.me.us/house/townlist.htm
To find members of the state house of representatives, go to
http://www.state.me.us/legis/senate/senators/directory/index.htm.

5 Making a Living

Mainers have always been hardworking people. They have had to be, because Maine can be a tough place to make a living. That has been especially true in the past few years as jobs in some parts of Maine have decreased. The northern parts of the state have been hit particularly hard. By the end of 2002, the unemployment rate for all of Maine was 4.4 percent, which was actually lower than the national average. But in remote Washington County, in the northeastern corner of the state, more than twice as many people—8.8 percent—were out of work.

Manufacturing

Manufacturing is the most important segment of the Maine economy. But in the past few years, the manufacturing industry has been badly hurt, all across Maine. In the 1950s, half of all Maine workers were employed in manufacturing, making wood products, textiles, and shoes. Today, only about

Tourism—especially around the coast—is an important industry in Maine.

Throughout the state's history, the shipyards of Maine have been an important part of the economy.

15 percent of Mainers work in the manufacturing sector—and that number will probably fall even lower in the years to come.

Wood products are the most important of Maine's manufactured goods. The state ships Christmas trees and wreaths, plywood, shingles, and even toothpicks all over the world. The most important of Maine's wood products is pulp and paper, which pays nearly 25 percent of Maine's manufacturing wages. This industry, too, is suffering, with mills closing and hundreds of workers losing their jobs.

One of the main reasons is foreign competition. Maine's

manufacturers must now compete with products from other countries—plywood from Canada, shoes from Brazil, textiles from Bangladesh—that are often much cheaper than the ones they make.

Beginning in the 1990s, the shipyards of Bath and Kittery laid off many employees. This decline in the shipbuilding industry did not happen because of competition from other countries. The problem was that, in a time of peace, the military was not ordering as many ships.

From the Land and Water

It might seem surprising that Maine, with its rocky soil and short growing season, has any agriculture at all. But farming is quite important in some parts of the state. Farms in different parts of the state produce oats, hay, and corn. Most of these crops are used to make food for livestock. Aroostook County produces potatoes and broccoli. The Augusta area is well-known for its apple farms. Other parts of Maine produce blueberries, cranberries, and maple syrup.

Maine does not have a very large mining industry, but there are some valuable mined products. The Pine Tree state has sand, gravel, and limestone, which are used in construction. Copper and zinc can be found in northern parts of Maine, but they are not usually mined in large quantities.

Maine's fishing industry is an important part of the economy. Since the first settlements, boats and ships have gone into Maine's inland and coastal waters to catch fish and crustaceans. The fishing industry also includes the people who clean, prepare, pack, and ship the fish and crustaceans throughout the country and around the world.

Recipe for Maine Blueberry Pudding

This traditional Maine recipe is simple to make and delicious. You can use any kind of blueberries, but if you can find the low-bush kind from Maine—either fresh or canned—you can give them a try.

Ingredients:
3 cups blueberries
1 teaspoon cinnamon
3/4 cup sugar
1/2 cup water
6 slices bread, with the crusts removed
Whipped cream

Mix together the blueberries, cinnamon, sugar, and water. Have an adult help you cook the mixture on the stove (over medium heat) for about 10 minutes.

Place the mixture and the bread in the pan in a serving dish, alternating layers of bread and blueberry mixture. Chill the pudding in the refrigerator for a few hours.

Just before serving, top the pudding with cream, and enjoy!

Maine's fishing industry brings in a lot of money for local businessees.

But lately, the stocks of ocean fish such as cod and haddock have decreased. The fishing authorities have cut back hard on the numbers of fish that commercial fishermen are allowed to catch. While this protects the fish populations, it has made it very difficult for many Maine's fishermen to make a living.

Interestingly, the lobster population has not declined. In fact, it has increased greatly. In the 1950s, Maine's yearly lobster catch was about 20 million pounds. But in 2002, it was 61 million pounds. This was worth more than $200 million to the Maine economy. Maine is famous for these tasty crustaceans. "Lobstering's hard work," says Theron Tweedie, a master boat and house builder in Spruce Head. "You'll head out at four o'clock in the morning, in all kinds of weather, and you might not [get] in till eight o'clock at night. But it's a good life, and you can make a good living."

Service and Tourism

The service industry includes any jobs that provide a service to others. Teachers, doctors, tour guides, bank tellers, waiters, and hotel clerks are all part of the service industry. The service industry employs a large number of Mainers.

Tourism is one of the most profitable parts of Maine's service industry. As important as the fishing and timber industries are, tourism is now the second-largest segment of the Maine economy. The Pine Tree State has something for just about every visitor. This includes the spectacular beauty of the seacoast, the unspoiled wilderness in the interior—including 436,064 square miles of national and state parks—and the peaceful, easygoing Maine way of life.

But what really brings tourists to Maine, more than anything else, is the people. Mainers offer visitors a friendly "down east" welcome that keeps them coming back, year after year. And that makes tourism one Maine industry that keeps growing, no matter how troubled the economy is.

New Ways

Maine still relies heavily on its traditional industries—especially its natural resources, such as wood and fish—but it is working hard to develop modern, advanced industries. Financial services have become an important part of the Maine economy, as banks and insurance companies have moved their headquarters into the state. More and more technology industries, such as software companies and Internet service providers, are moving into Maine, especially around Portland.

There are many reasons these businesses are choosing to come to Maine. The state has a pretty low cost of living, which means that some parts are not too expensive to live in. Maine also has excellent communications and technology. The state also has good transportation facilities, including two international airports, and a high-speed ferry to Canada. These all make Maine a good place for international businesses to locate. But what is really bringing these new industries and employers to the state is the Maine work force. Many Mainers are well-educated and highly skilled, and they are known for their hard work.

People have always had to work hard just to get by in Maine, often taking on more than one job to get by. A fisherman would often work as a carpenter in the winter, when it was too cold to go out on the water. A farmer might have a job "in town," to help make ends meet. This tradition of hard work and resourcefulness continues to this day, and it is perfectly natural for a Mainer to have more than one occupation.

It is this spirit—hardworking, independent, and resourceful—that has always carried Mainers through good times and bad. And it is this spirit that makes the people of Maine by far the state's most important natural resource.

Products & Resources

Tourism

More than nine million visitors come to Maine every year. That is almost nine times the state's population. With the state's thriving cities, museums, historical sites, coastal resorts, inland parks and scenic areas Maine tourists have a lot to choose from. Tourism is the state's second-largest employer.

Potatoes

Maine is the third-largest potato-growing state in the country. Almost 70,000 acres of Maine farmland —mostly in Aroostook County—produce nearly $280 million worth of potatoes every year.

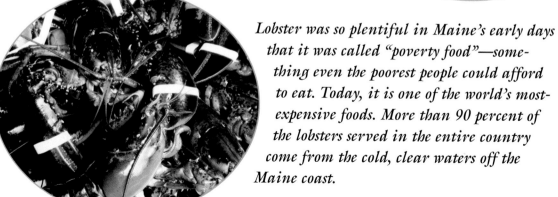

Lobster

Lobster was so plentiful in Maine's early days that it was called "poverty food"—something even the poorest people could afford to eat. Today, it is one of the world's most-expensive foods. More than 90 percent of the lobsters served in the entire country come from the cold, clear waters off the Maine coast.

Blueberries

Wild "low-bush" blueberries—smaller and more flavorful than the kind that are grown on farms—grow beautifully in Maine's thin, rocky soil. The state produces 74.5 million pounds of them every year.

Pulp and Paper

Manufacturing is the largest sector of Maine's economy. Wood products—from sailboats to toothpicks and everything in between—are an important part of the manufacturing industry. Paper made from Maine's trees—and turned into the world's books and newspapers—is worth billions of dollars to Maine's economy every year.

Dairy Farms

At one time, Maine had more than 5,000 dairy farms throughout the state. Today, however, there are only about 350. But this does not mean that the products from these farms are not important to Maine. The milk from Maine's dairy cows is made into cream, butter, ice cream, and cheese. Dairy farmers also use their cows' manure as part of rich fertilizers that are sold throughout the state and around the country.

The Maine state flag—chosen in 1909—shows the state seal, against a blue background. The background is the same shade of blue as in the flag of the United States

The state seal shows many of the people and resources that have been important throughout Maine's history. A farmer and a sailor stand on either side of a shield with a pine tree and a moose. Above the shield is the state's motto, "Dirigo," which means "I lead." Below is the word "Maine."

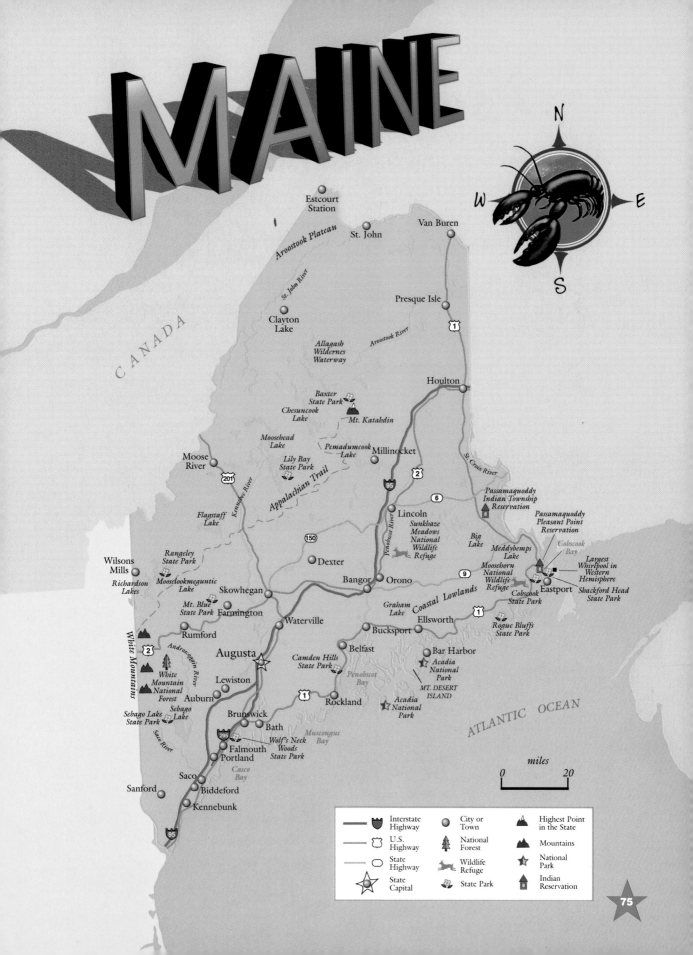

MAINE

N
W · E
S

Estcourt
Station

St. John

Van Buren

Aroostook Plateau

Presque Isle
🛡 1

St. John River

Clayton
Lake

*Allagash
Wilderness
Waterway*

Aroostook River

CANADA

Houlton

Baxter
State Park 🌸
*Chesuncook
Lake*
🌳 Mt. Katahdin

*Moosehead
Lake*

*Pemadumcook
Lake*
Millinocket

St. Croix River

Moose
River
🛡 201

Lily Bay
State Park

Appalachian Trail

Kennebec River

🛡 95
U.S. 2

Lincoln

6

Passamaquoddy
Indian Township
Reservation 🏠

Flagstaff
Lake

150

Penobscot River

Sunkhaze
Meadows
National
Wildlife
Refuge 🦌

Big
Lake

Meddybemps
Lake

Passamaquoddy
Pleasant Point
Reservation

*Cobscook
Bay*

Wilsons
Mills

Rangeley
State Park

Dexter

Moosehorn
National
Wildlife
Refuge 🦌

Largest
Whirlpool
in Western
Hemisphere

*Richardson
Lakes*

*Mooselookmeguntic
Lake*

Bangor
Orono

9

Cobscook
State Park
🏠 Eastport

Shackford Head
State Park

Skowhegan

Mt. Blue
State Park
Farmington

*Graham
Lake*

Coastal Lowlands

Ellsworth

1

Rumford
🛡 2

Waterville

Bucksport

Rogue Bluffs
State Park

White Mountains

Androscoggin River

⭐ Augusta

Belfast

Bar Harbor
⭐ Acadia
National
Park

White
Mountain
National
Forest ⛰️

Lewiston

Camden Hills
State Park
*Penobscot
Bay*

MT. DESERT
ISLAND

Auburn

1

*Sebago Lake
State Park*
*Sebago
Lake*

Brunswick
Bath

Rockland

Acadia ⭐
National
Park

Saco River

🛡 295
Falmouth
Portland

Wolf's Neck
Woods
State Park

*Muscongus
Bay*

ATLANTIC OCEAN

Sanford

Saco

*Casco
Bay*

Biddeford
Kennebunk

🛡 95

miles
0   20

Legend

Symbol	Description	Symbol	Description	Symbol	Description
🛡	Interstate Highway	🔵	City or Town	⛰️	Highest Point in the State
⬡	U.S. Highway	🌳	National Forest	🏔️	Mountains
◯	State Highway	🦌	Wildlife Refuge	⭐	National Park
⭐	State Capital	🏕️	State Park	🏠	Indian Reservation

State of Maine Song

Words and Music by Roger Vinton Snow

Grand State of Maine, _____

proud - ly we sing _____ To

tell your glo - ries to the land, _____ To

shout your prais - es till the ech - oes ring. _____

Should fate un - kind _____

send us to roam, _____ The

scent of the fra - grant pines, _____ the tang of the salt - y sea Will

call us home. _____

76

State Song

More About Maine

Books

DeFord, Deborah. *Maine, the Pine Tree State*. Milwaukee, WI: World Almanac Library, 2003.

Dornfeld, Margaret. *Maine*. Tarrytown, NY: Benchmark Books, 2001.

Graham, Amy. *Maine*. Berkeley Heights, NJ: My ReportLinks.com, 2002.

Web Sites

Maine Office of Tourism
http://www.visitmaine.com

Maine State Librarian - Ask a Librarian
http://www.maine.gov/msl/services/ask.htm

Secretary of State's Kids' Page
http://www.state.me.us/sos/kids

About the Author

Terry Allan Hicks has written books for Marshall Cavendish about the states of New Hampshire and Nevada. He lives in Connecticut with his wife, Nancy, and their children, Jamie, Jack, and Andrew.

Index

Page numbers in **boldface** are illustrations.